TAP DANCING

LISA DILLMAN

Heinemann Library
Chicago, Illinois

Photo research by Jill Birschbach
Designed by Joanna Turner
Originated by Ambassador Litho Ltd.
Printed in China by WKT Company Ltd.

10 09 08 07 06
10 9 8 7 6 5 4 3 2 1

Library of Congress Cataloging-in-Publication Data

Dillman, Lisa, 1957-
  Tap dancing / by Lisa Dillman.
     v. cm. — (Get going! hobbies)
  Contents: What is tap dancing? — Tapping history — Tapping in: getting started — Dressing for tap — Warming up — Getting the body in place — Creating a single sound — Creating multiple sounds — Using your whole body — Performing for an audience — Tap dancing meets the street — Tapping today.
  ISBN 1-4034-6120-1 (Hardcover) — ISBN 1-4034-6127-9 (Paperback)
  1. Tap dancing—Juvenile literature. [1. Tap dancing.] I. Title. II. Series.
  GV1794.D56 2004
  792.7'8—dc22

                                2003025499

Acknowledgments
The author and publisher are grateful to the following for permission to reproduce copyright material: p. 4t Adams Eddie/Corbis Sygma; pp. 4b, 29 Hulton Archive/Getty Images; p. 5 David Young-Wolff/Photo Edit; p. 6t Robert Lifson/Heinemann Library; pp. 6b, 28b Robbie Jack/Corbis; p. 7t Warner Brothers/The Kobal Collection/Picture Desk; p. 7b Columbia/The Kobal Collection/Picture Desk; p. 8 The Kobal Collection/Picture Desk; p. 9 Norbert Schaefer/Corbis; pp. 11, 12, 13, 14, 15, 16, 17, 18, 19, 20, 21, 23 Greg Williams/Heinemann Library; p. 25 John Springer Collection/Corbis; p. 26t Bettmann/Corbis; p. 26b Corbis; p. 27 Tri-Star/The Kobal Collection/Picture Desk; p. 28t Ron Frehm/AP Wide World Photo

Cover photograph of tap dancers by Ash Knotek/Snappers/Zuma Press/Newscom

Special thanks to Whitney Moncrief, a dance instructor at Hubbard Street Dance Chicago, for her comments that were used to complete this book.

Every effort has been made to contact copyright holders of any material reproduced in this book. Any omissions will be rectified in subsequent printings if notice is given to the publisher.

CONTENTS

What Is Tap Dancing? 4

Tapping History 6

Tapping In: Getting Started 8

Dressing for Tap. 10

Warming Up 12

Getting the Body in Place. 14

Creating a Single Sound. 16

Creating More Single Sounds 18

Creating Multiple Sounds. 20

Using Your Whole Body 22

Performing for an Audience 24

Tap Dancing Meets the Street 26

Tapping Today. 28

Glossary *30*

More Books to Read *31*

Taking It Further *31*

Index *32*

Some words are shown in bold, **like this.** You can find out what they mean by looking in the glossary.

Tap is a style of **percussive dance.** The dancers wear special shoes with metal **taps** that make sounds when they touch the floor. They create rhythms with their feet as if they are drumming on the floor. Tap is an unusual dance form because it depends on being heard as well as seen.

For example, compare tap dance to ballet. Ballet dancers move silently to the music. Tap dancers, however, accompany music with rhythms. You can hear the rhythms the dancers create with their steps.

TWO FORMS OF TAP

There are two main forms of tap dancing. In Broadway or chorus line tap, a large group of dancers taps out a rhythm. The look and feel of this type of dancing depends on all the dancers being **in step,** or moving in the same way at the same time.

The world famous Rockettes often perform at New York City's Radio City Music Hall. Their routine features simple tap steps performed by a long line of dancers.

In the other type of tap—jazz tap or rhythm tap— the idea is to create music with your feet. The best tap dancers can tap their feet as fast as great drummers can move their hands. This type of tap dance began long ago and is still popular today.

In the 1920s and 1930s, Bill "Bojangles" Robinson thrilled stage and film audiences with his expert tap moves.

WHERE TO LEARN AND PRACTICE

This book tells you how to begin to learn tap dancing. It shows you some basic steps and tells you how to perform them. But learning dance is not like learning math. To learn how to tap dance, you have to get on your feet and practice. To do that safely, you will have to take lessons.

Early in the history of tap dance, dancers entertained people on the street and even challenged one another to dancing contests. Children learned by watching the more experienced dancers. Today most students learn by taking classes at a **dance studio.**

TEACHERS OF TAP

You will need a good teacher—someone with a background in tap dancing who can watch your progress and help you improve your steps. You will start out in a beginner's class. You and your fellow tappers will learn basic moves and combinations. When you train in a group, you can learn from your teacher and by watching and talking to others. The more you learn, the more you can begin to create dance **routines** of your own.

Tap classes provide a great way to get you going with your new hobby. They also give you a place to make new friends.

TAPPING HISTORY

Tap dance traces its roots to West African **stomp dances** in which barefoot dancers stomp out rhythms to the beat of drums. These dances began long ago and are still performed today.

These students are learning traditional African dances from the teacher in front of them.

Dancers in many African **cultures** use a **traditional** shuffling step and keep their feet close to the ground. They say that this helps them to hear the rhythm of life and to feel the spiritual power of Earth. This **shuffle step** is also one of the most basic steps in tap dancing.

Hundreds of years ago, thousands of people from Africa were forced to be slaves in North America. They brought African music and dance traditions with them. They created rhythms using dried cow bones and spoons and used chanting to imitate drumbeats. They also clapped their hands and tapped out rhythms with their feet.

BLENDING TRADITIONS

As African people came into contact with other cultures in North America, they shared their dances. African Americans danced as a form of entertainment for themselves. Over time, new dance forms developed. No one is exactly sure how tap developed, but many believe that the form began when African stomp dancing was blended with Irish step dancing.

Riverdance is a modern showcase for traditional Irish step dancing. This popular show began in Ireland and has been performed all over the world.

TAP DANCE ON THE STAGE AND SCREEN

By the 1930s, tap dancing had become an important part of **vaudeville,** a type of stage show that featured singers, dancers, and **comedians.** Audiences were amazed by the speed and **athleticism** of vaudeville tap dancers. But as Broadway musicals and movies became popular, a different kind of tap began to develop. Dancers did not **improvise,** or make up their own steps. Instead they followed the directions of a **choreographer.** Each step was carefully planned and rehearsed.

The 1933 movie Footlight Parade *gave actor James Cagney a chance to show off his years of vaudeville training.*

MODERN TAP

Improvisational tap dance continued in smaller **venues** such as jazz music clubs. However, in the late 1950s rock and roll music became popular. Tap dancing did not blend well with the sound of rock music. Its popularity faded until the 1970s, when tap was revived. A whole new group of dancers became interested in learning how to tap. Some of the world's best tap dancers taught their moves to younger dancers, and the tap tradition continued. Today tap is still popular with kids and adults alike.

Gregory Hines (1946–2003) had a huge influence on modern tap dance.

Sit still for a moment and listen. What do you hear? The sound of your own breathing? The beating of your heart? The ticking of a clock? The dripping of a faucet? Our world is full of rhythms. At any given time, the rhythm of life is going on all around us. Each person has his or her own rhythms inside. Your rhythms are a part of who you are. Tap dancing is a way to bring those rhythms out for everyone to see and hear!

LEARNING THE BASICS

With the help of a good teacher, it does not take long to learn a few tap dance basics. Each step is made up of movements you use in your daily life. In fact, the most basic step in tap uses movements just like those you use for walking! Once you learn the basic steps, you can put them together in different combinations to create tap **routines** with many different sounds and rhythm patterns.

Fred Astaire became famous for his exciting dance routines that were featured in many Hollywood movies. He started studying tap dancing when he was five years old.

TAPPING YOUR SKILLS

Keep one thing in mind: Tap dancing is not about the shoes. It is about expressing your **personality.** Sure, the shoes will help you make cool sounds and rhythm patterns. But without you and your inner rhythms, those shoes would just sit quietly in a corner.

PREPARING TO LEARN

Tap dancers need good balance and control. They must develop their strength, reflexes, and body awareness. Before you begin your tap training, think about the things you do well.

- Are you a good runner? Tap dancing requires quickness and **stamina.**

- Are you a high jumper? Jumping is an important part of tap dancing.

- Can you skate or ski? The balance you need for these activities will come in handy in tap dancing.

- Do you play a musical instrument? Music, like tap dancing, requires a strong sense of rhythm.

Even if you do not have these skills, you can still be a great tap dancer. The important thing to remember is that you probably already have some of the skills that will help you succeed as a dancer.

Exercising regularly will help prepare you for learning how to tap dance.

DRESSING FOR TAP

You may have seen old movies in which tap dancers dressed in top hats and tuxedos. But tap dancers today perform in all kinds of different clothing. You do not need special clothing or equipment. Wear loose-fitting clothes to class, but make sure your pants are not so loose that they get in your way. Your pant legs should not drag on the floor because that could cause you to trip.

Your early lessons will mostly have to do with weight placement and body positions. In fact, when you first begin taking tap lessons, your teacher will probably ask you not to wear tap shoes. You are likely to come down too hard on your feet to achieve sounds rather than learning how to make the sounds happen through rhythm and timing. The beginning stages of tap dancing are less about making noise and more about finding your rhythm.

SAFETY TIPS

As with all sports and dance forms, it is important that you follow these simple safety rules.

- To keep your hair out of your eyes, pin it back or wear a headband.

- If you wear glasses, secure them with a sports band, which are available at sporting goods stores.

- Keep your fingernails clean and trimmed.

- Always warm up properly before you begin your dance practice.

- **If you feel pain or shortness of breath, stop what you are doing immediately.**

CHOOSING THE RIGHT SHOES

Although it is likely that you will begin your tap training in regular shoes, eventually you will have to purchase a pair of tap shoes. These are usually fairly strong leather shoes with double soles. The shoes must then be fitted with pieces of metal called **taps,** which are screwed into the heel and toe. The taps make a sharp cracking sound when they strike the floor. Some shoes come with the taps already installed, but most do not. Taps are usually installed by a professional shoe-repair person.

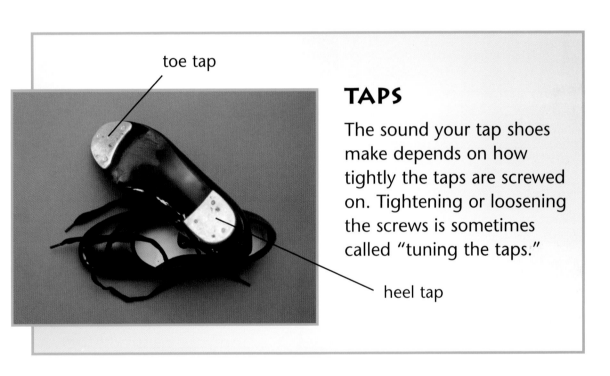

toe tap

TAPS

The sound your tap shoes make depends on how tightly the taps are screwed on. Tightening or loosening the screws is sometimes called "tuning the taps."

heel tap

Make sure your tap shoes fit well. They should be snug but never tight. You will be doing a lot of stomping and other foot movements when you tap. Shoes that do not fit could cause trouble!

WARMING UP

Before you try out new tap dance movements or take part in a class, you should always warm up your muscles.

You can warm up your whole body by running in place for a few minutes. But you will want to spend some extra time warming up your hips, calves, and feet.

WARMING UP YOUR HIPS

1 Lie on your back on a mat or the floor.

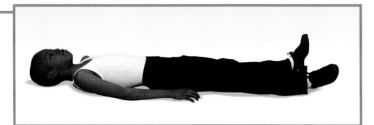

2 Bend your legs, and tuck your knees up toward your chest.

3 With your arms extended straight out to your sides and your palms on the floor, roll your hips first to the left and then to the right.

4 Try to keep your back flat on the floor. Do not strain. If you feel any pain, stop the movement right away.

5 Do this ten times on each side.

WARMING UP YOUR CALVES

1 Sit on the floor with your legs straight out in front of you.

2 Stretch your calf muscles by pointing your toes toward the floor.

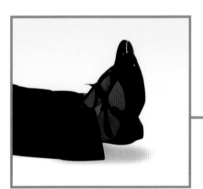

3 You should feel a gentle pull and a good stretch. Hold this position for five seconds.

4 Flex your toes back toward you and hold this position for five seconds. You should feel a stretch on the backs of your legs.

5 Repeat these movements ten times.

WARMING UP YOUR FEET

One way to prepare your feet for a tap workout is to give each foot a short massage.

1 Sit on the floor and grab one foot.

2 With your thumb, rub the bottom of your foot in small circles.

3 Use as much pressure as feels comfortable. Use your fingers to massage the top and sides of your foot. Do this for several minutes.

GETTING THE BODY IN PLACE

When it comes to learning tap dancing moves, what do you think are the most important parts of your body? If you are like most beginners, you will probably answer, "My feet." But the truth is your hips are the parts of your body that are most important for those tricky tap moves.

In tap, as in almost any dance form, the hips provide the engine for most movements. When tap dancers are perfectly balanced they say they are "over their hips." This means their hips are in position to move their feet and take them in any direction.

Always make sure you are properly balanced before you attempt any dance steps or routines.

ALIGNMENT AND BALANCE

Before you get started on basic tap steps on the next few pages, try this simple exercise for body **alignment** and balance.

1 Stand up straight with your body relaxed and your feet flat on the floor.

2 Place your weight evenly on both your feet.

3 Now imagine that your upper body is being pulled straight up from your hips. Make yourself as tall as possible

4 Rock on the balls of your feet and lift your heels off the floor.

5 Stay in this position while you count to 30.

6 Slowly lower your heels to the floor.

FINDING BALANCE

You might have a hard time keeping your balance the first few times you try this. But remember that tap dancing is all about balance and control. If you do this exercise a few times each day, you will be able to hold the position longer and longer. That will help as you continue to work on your tap steps.

When you do this exercise, start out slowly so you do not slip and fall.

Tap's basic steps form a simple dance vocabulary. Once you know the steps, you can combine them in all kinds of ways to make different patterns. Here are some of the basic moves you will learn as a beginner. Your teacher may have different names for these steps, depending on where you live.

BASIC TAP STEPS

Step: Shift your weight from one foot to the other as you do when you walk. Carry your weight forward on the balls of your feet. You can step in any direction. This move is also sometimes called a *single.*

Stamp: Do a *step* (single) but come down on both your heel and your toe at the same time. In other words, keep your foot flat when it hits the floor and then transfer your weight to your other foot.

Stomp: This move is just like a *stamp* except that you do not transfer your weight to your other foot. The sound your foot makes hitting the floor should be loud and solid.

Touch: This move makes a sound like a *step.* It uses the ball of the foot. The difference is that there is no transfer of weight from one foot to the other.

Brush: In a *brush,* the front part of your foot leaves the floor in a forward motion. You can create sounds with this move with the ball of your foot and with the surfaces of the toe **taps.**

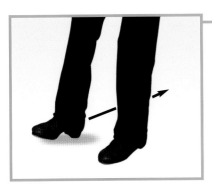

Back Brush: This move is the same as a *brush* except that your foot strikes the floor with a backward motion. This step is also sometimes called a *back.*

Scuff: This move is like a *brush* but you hit the floor with your heel.

Heel: In this move, you simply drop the heel of the foot that is carrying your weight.

Heel Drop: In this move, you drop the heel of the foot that is not carrying your weight.

Heel Step: In this move, you step onto the heel while forcefully transferring your weight.

Toe: To do this move, you drop the toe of the foot that is carrying your weight.

Toe Drop: This move is just like the toe move except that you drop the toe of the foot that is not carrying your weight.

Hop: In this move, you hop on the ball of one foot without transferring your weight to the other.

Hamp: To do this move, perform the *hop* move with your foot flat.

Jump: This is a landing move. You land on the balls of both feet. Your feet can be together or apart.

Slide: Tap dancers use this move to travel across the floor. One foot slides the body across the floor in any direction.

CREATING MULTIPLE SOUNDS

Once you have mastered some individual steps, you will be ready to try some moves that create two sounds or more. After that, you can put three sounds together. Soon you will be making up your own combinations!

TWO-SOUND COMBINATIONS

A combination movement is written with a slash between each individual move. For example, *step/brush* or *back/brush.*

Double: To perform a *double,* you do a *brush* and then a *step* or a *back brush* followed by a *step.* Listen to the sound your feet make on the floor.

Ball Change: The *ball change* is a rocking movement of two quick steps using the same weight-bearing leg. You can perform a *ball change* to the front, sides, or back. For example, step/stamp or heel drop/heel.

Roll: For this combination, you do a *step* followed by a *heel* (step/heel).

THREE-SOUND COMBINATIONS

You now have enough steps to make some great rhythms when you put three sounds together. Here are a couple of relatively simple combinations. These steps alternate from one foot to the other.

Basic Drawback: Start slowly. Do a *slow brush* followed by a *heel* followed by a *step* (brush/heel/step). When you feel you have mastered the three movements, increase the speed and do them as a combination.

Three-Point Crawl: If you continue to study tap, you will find out that there are a few different *crawl* movements. This is the simplest one. It is made up of a step/heel/toe combination. You perform this move with one leg turned in.

Experienced tap dancers can move their bodies in one rhythm while using their feet to tap out a very different one. The dancer might tap in time to one line of the music while the head, arms, neck, and torso create a counterpoint, or a completely independent rhythm.

In the beginning of your tap study, you may have to concentrate very hard on your hips, legs, and feet. It is easy to forget that dance is a whole-body activity. But there are a few simple tricks you can use to loosen up the rest of your body.

LOOSENING UP

The number one rule is: stay loose! Stiff hands, a tight neck, or a frozen facial expression can really spoil the look of tap dancing. When you are getting ready to tap, give yourself a moment or two to relax.

- Loosen your jaw by opening your mouth and moving your lower jaw from side to side a few times. This will help you avoid clenching your teeth.

- Roll your neck to get rid of extra neck and shoulder tension. Just roll your head forward, to one side, to the back, and to the other side. Do not go too fast.

- Open and close your fists a few times if your hands feel tight. Hold your hands out in front of your body and shake them.

- Shrug your shoulders a few times. This can help loosen up tight shoulder and neck muscles.

- Arch your back and then bend forward at the waist and try to touch the floor with your fingertips.

Now try a simple tap routine using your hands and a combination of the steps you have learned. As you complete each step, clap your hands together twice. Keep your shoulders and hands loose. You are going to do a *bombershay* followed by a *ball change.* Here are the basic moves:

With the right foot: *step* (clap, clap)/*back* (clap, clap)/*heel step* (clap, clap)/

With the left foot: *step* (clap, clap)/*stamp* (clap, clap)/*heel drop* (clap, clap)

1 Begin very slowly.

2 When you feel you have mastered the movements, increase your speed.

3 If you feel tension in your shoulders, neck, hands, or face, stop the movement and start over. The goal is to stay as loose as possible.

4 Try to do at least three rounds of this combination.

Bombershay: You make this three-sound move by doing a *step* followed by a *back* followed by a *heel step* (step/back/heel step). Go through this combination very slowly a few times. When you feel you can do it perfectly in slow motion, gradually begin to increase the speed. The photos below show the sequence of steps from left to right.

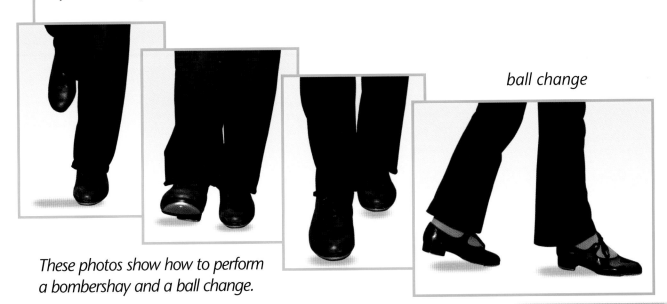

ball change

These photos show how to perform a bombershay and a ball change.

If you stick with tap dancing, eventually you will want to perform in front of an audience. When that time comes, your teacher may set up an individual or group **recital.** This performance, usually for friends and family, is to showcase your skills and the progress you have made.

Here are a few tips to help you get the most from your performance.

1 Before the performance, warm up your muscles just as you would before a class.

2 Do not eat anything just before your performance. Dancing with a full stomach can lead to stomach pain.

3 Drink plenty of water before and after the performance.

4 Many dancers have "butterflies,"a fluttery feeling in the pit of the stomach, before they perform. If you have this feeling, just remember that it is excitement. Take deep breaths and focus on giving the best performance you can.

5 Pay attention backstage. You do not want to miss your entrance!

6 If you make a mistake, do not worry about it. Keep dancing.

7 Do the best you can, and have fun!

DEVELOPING STAGE PRESENCE

Some tap dancers make even the most difficult movements look easy. They seem relaxed. They take joy in their dancing. Others may be able to do the steps perfectly, but there is still something missing.

What makes a person a great performer? The answer is **stage presence.** You can tell when performers have it. You want to watch them. You cannot take your eyes off them. The more stage presence the performer has, the more connected the audience feels to him or her. The more connected the audience feels, the more it gives back to the performer in attention, **admiration,** and applause.

Presence has a lot to do with confidence. It comes from giving 100 percent when you are onstage. And the way to get more confidence when you tap dance is to practice. The more you practice, the better you will dance. The better you dance, the more stage presence you are likely to have.

Sammy Davis, Jr., was a multitalented performer who had not only great technical dancing skills, but also remarkable stage presence.

Like the dances of the ancient Africans, modern tap dance is often based on **improvisation.** This means the dancer performs by making up combinations of steps along the way. The dancer becomes a musician as well as a dancer, using imagination and rhythm to express original ideas and emotions.

In the early part of the 20th century, many young tap dancers learned their moves by practicing alone or in small groups on street corners. They danced for their own entertainment and for people passing by.

BREAK DANCING

These days you are not likely to see tap dancers on street corners. But there is still a strong street-dance tradition in many cities. In the 1980s break dancing became popular in New York City and soon the craze spread around the country. This wild **acrobatic** dance form uses spins, kicks, jumps, and turns. In fact, it uses many steps and movements from other dance forms, including tap.

Tap dancing and break dancing share some of the same steps.

Legendary tap dancer Bunny Briggs started dancing as a little boy. He danced for tips on the streets of Harlem in New York.

CHALLENGE DANCES

Both break-dancers and tap dancers sometimes compete to see which performer can come up with the most exciting routine. These competitions show off the speed, strength, and coordination of each dancer among rivals. They are called **challenge dances.**

The challenge dance grew out of an old African **tradition.** It has always been an important part of rhythm tap dancing, break dancing, and other popular dance forms. In modern challenge dances all over the world, dancers form a circle and begin tapping or chanting a rhythm. Then one dancer at a time goes into the middle of the circle and shows off his or her best moves.

These competitions offer dancers the chance to learn new steps and combinations. Because each dancer is **unique,** even identical steps can seem very different from one dancer to the next.

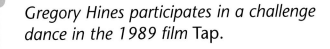

Gregory Hines participates in a challenge dance in the 1989 film Tap.

TAPPING TODAY

TAP IS HERE TO STAY!

Through the years tap dancing's popularity has gone up and down. It was very popular in the 1930s and 1940s, but faded during the 1950s and 1960s. Then in the 1970s there was renewed interest. Today tap is still going strong.

Many of today's tap dancers perform in a style that blends tap with various types of street dancing. One of the best-known modern tap dancers is Savion Glover, star of the popular musical Bring in 'Da Noise, Bring in 'Da Funk.

The Tap Dogs, shown here, are a very successful group of tap dancers from Australia.

TAP GOES ELECTRONIC

A dancer named Alfred Desio developed electronic **taps** called Tap-Tronics. With this technology he can turn tap dancing into electronic music. He inserts a device between the tap and the sole of the dancer's shoe. As the dancer performs, the device sends signals to a **synthesizer** that makes each step sound like squeals, a crash, an echo, musical notes, and even voices!

Many dance professionals feel that such electronic devices could be the future of tap. They believe that the wide variety of electronic sounds and new techniques will bring more and more young people to the art form.

Tap dance has evolved over hundreds of years. From Africa to the streets and stages of New York City to **dance studios** all over the world, it is an art form that continues to progress.

Fred Astaire filmed a scene in the 1951 film Royal Wedding *in which he appeared to tap dance on the ceiling and walls of a hotel room.*

GLOSSARY

acrobatic   able to do athletic feats well, such as tumbling, balancing, jumping, and swinging from things

admiration   feeling of approval

alignment   how body parts are arranged in relation to other body parts

athletic   of or relating to athletes or athletics, which are games, sports, and exercises requiring strength and skill

challenge dance   dance tradition in which dancers challenge one another to perform their best steps

choreographer   creator of dance compositions and ballets

comedian   comical person, especially one who makes a living from comedy

culture   stage, form, or kind of civilization

dance studio   school or business that offers dance classes

improvisation   spontaneous creation and performance of dance steps

in step   in dance, identical steps by a group of dancers at the same time

percussive dance   dance that creates audible rhythms that accompany the music or become the musical accompaniment

personality   emotions and behavior that make one person different from another

recital   public performance by dance or music students

routine   series of dance steps worked out in advance that can be repeated again and again

shuffle step   dance step used in traditional African dances and tap dance

stage presence   charisma or charm of a person who performs for an audience

stamina   energy and staying power

stomp dance   traditional African dance in which dancers stomp out a rhythm to the beat of a drum

synthesizer   computer that produces and controls sound

taps   metal plates on the toes and heels of tap shoes that make a sharp clicking noise when they strike the floor

tradition   handing down of beliefs, customs, or information from one generation to the next

unique   special, different from all others

vaudeville   early 20th-century stage entertainment that featured music, dance, and comedy skits

venue   place or location

MORE BOOKS TO READ

Coffey, Judith. *Ballet, Tap and All That Jazz!* Jonesboro, Ark.: Rainbow Educational Concepts, 1998.

Glover, Savion, and Bruce Weber. *Savion!: My Life in Tap.* New York: HarperCollins Children's Book Group, 2000.

Hebach, Susan. *Tap Dancing.* Danbury, Conn.: Scholastic Library Publishing, 2001.

TAKING IT FURTHER

American Tap Dance Foundation
33 Little West 12th Street
Suite 105B
New York, NY 10014-1313
(646) 230-9564
info@atdf.org

International Tap Association
P.O. Box 356
Boulder, CO 80306
(303) 443-7989
ita@tapdance.org

National Dance Education Organization
4948 St. Elmo Avenue, Suite 301
Bethesda, MD 20814
(301) 657-2880
info@ndeo.org

National Tap Ensemble
P.O. Box 2439
Hagerstown, MD 21741-2439
(888) NTE-TAPS
staff@usatap.org

INDEX

African cultures 6, 27
alignment 15
associations 31
Astaire, Fred 8, 29
athleticism 7
audience, performing in front of an 24, 25

balance 9, 14, 15
ballet 4
basic tap steps 16–19
   back brush 17, 20
   brush 17, 20, 21
   hamp 19
   heel 17, 20, 21
   heel drop 18
   heel step 18, 23
   hop 19
   jump 19
   scuff 17
   slide 19
   stamp 16
   step (single) 16, 20, 21, 23
   stomp 16
   toe 18
   toe drop 18
   touch 16
   see also combination movements
body awareness 9
bombershay 23
break dancing 26, 27
Briggs, Bunny 26
Broadway (chorus line) tap 4

Cagney, James 7
challenge dances 27
choreographers 7
classes 5, 10
clothing 10
combination movements 20–21

ball change 20, 23
basic drawback 21
bombershay 23
double 20
roll 20
three-point crawl 21
three-sound combinations 21, 23
two-sound combinations 20
   see also basic tap steps
confidence 25
control 9, 15

dance studios 5
dancing in step 4
Davis, Sammy, Jr. 25
Desio, Alfred 29

electronic taps 29
exercise 9
   alignment and balance 15
   loosening up 22
   warming up 12–13

Glover, Savion 28

Hines, Gregory 7, 27
hips 12, 14
history of tap dance 6–7

improvisation 7, 26
Irish step dancing 6

jazz tap (rhythm tap) 4
jumping 9, 19

loosening up exercises 22

movies and musicals 7

percussive dance 4

performance 24–25
personality 9
popularity of tap dancing 7, 28

rhythm 4, 6, 8, 9, 10, 22
Robinson, Bill ("Bojangles") 4
Rockettes 4
routines 5, 8

safety 10
shoes 4, 10, 11
   electronic taps 29
   taps 4, 11
shuffle step 6
stage presence 25
stamina 9
stomp dances 6
street-dance tradition 26

Tap-Tronics 29
taps 4, 11
   electronic taps 29
tuning 11
teachers 5, 6, 8, 10

vaudeville 7

warming up exercises 12–13